APPLE AIRTAG USER GU

THE ULTIMATE BEGINNER'S MANUAL TO USING THE LATEST APPLE AIRTAG EASILY WITH TIPS AND TRICKS

BY

FELIX O. COLLINS

Contents

INTRODUCTION

After years of rumors and speculation, Apple unveiled the much-anticipated AirTag in April 2021. Small round tags are designed to be attached to items such as keys and wallets so that these apps can be tracked in the "Find Me" app via the Bluetooth device next to the Apple device.

Apple AirTag is a small button-built tool designed to link to items such as keys and wallets so that these apps can be hunted down using Apple-enabled Bluetooth on Apple's "Find Me" app.

If you have a new AirTag, you need to set it up and set it up for use. Before performing this operation, please be sure to update your iPhone or iPad to iOS 14.5 or iPadOS 14.5 respectively. You can check your iOS version in Settings -> General -> Software Updates.

Features

AirTag Reviews

Before launching AirTag, members of the media can check it out, and the first impression is good. For AirTags in the Apple ecosystem, AirTags is described as "smart" and "powerful", and its accuracy is praised for its tracking capabilities.

Sometimes it can take a full 30 seconds or more to get the original AirTag position from another room, and due to Bluetooth and other reasons, the inaccurate location can be frustrated by obstacles and walls. Accurate tracking of U1 can help solve this problem.

Be sure to check out our full summary for more details.

AirTags design

AirTag is a small, button-shaped, white-button front-facing tracker, which can be customized with engraved and silver support. AirTag is designed for a CR2032 internal battery and requires additional accessories to connect to the item.

The AirTag is 1.26 inches wide and 0.31 inches high (8 mm). It weighs 0.39 ounces (11 grams).

AirTag recording

Each AirTag can write up to four characters or emoji characters, but due to size limitations, most emojis also have some limitations. Due to Apple's content filtering, certain emoji threads and phrases are also banned.

For example, you can't pair emoji with "horse face" and "poop" emoji, and you can't use curse words.

AirTags activity

AirTag has been added and managed in the "Find My" program under the "Item" tab launched by Apple on iOS 14.3. Like other Apple devices, each AirTag is displayed on the "Find my app" app, so you can see where it is. AirTag connects to your iOS and macOS devices via Bluetooth.

Apple adds a U1 chip to each AirTag, so you can see its exact location inside the house or outside (if not nearby), or in a nearby known location (if not). There is a built-in audio player to locate the lost AirTag in the house, you can play the sound with the "Find My" program, or you can ask Siri to find the noisy AirTag.

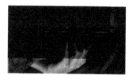

If AirTag is lost or stolen, the "Find My" network can help you find it. "Find My Network" uses hundreds of millions of iPhone, iPad, and Mac devices to help you find AirTag. When AirTag is detected on someone else's device, it will be displayed on a map.

In "Lost Mode", when someone in the "People who found me" network finds AirTag, it will automatically send a notification, you can add your contact details so that the person who found your item can contact you.

Accurate search

iPhones with a U1 chip (including iPhone 11 and iPhone 12 models) can take advantage of the Precision Finding feature, which allows you to view specific instructions on how to recover lost AirTag. Direct search includes AR, audible sound, and touch feedback to help you.

Replace missing AirTag

If you encounter a lost AirTag, or someone encounters a lost Air-Tag, you can scan it with any NFC-installed smartphone to display contact details.

This applies to iPhone and Android devices, so when you find something, scan it to find the owner. If it is in "Lost" mode, Air-Tag will re-transfer its location to the owner via the "Find Mine" network.

AirTags battery

AirTags uses a non-removable CR2032 battery, which is designed to last for up to a year before it needs to be replaced. The user can replace the battery, and to add another battery, you can press and twist the AirTag back panel to remove it.

If your AirTag battery is low, you will be notified that the battery needs to be replaced.

AirTag charging

There is no need to charge AirTag because Apple designed the CR2032 batteries that can be replaced by the user.

AirTags range

Apple did not provide detailed information about the AirTag distance, but the maximum Bluetooth distance is approximately 100 meters, so AirTag should be able to track at least that distance. Finding more detailed information will require further testing.

AirTags water resistance

AirTag has an IP67 waterproof and dust-free rating, which means it can withstand 30 minutes of immersion in up to one meter (3.3 meters) under laboratory conditions. This means that AirTag can effectively withstand exposure to rainwater or accidental spillage.

AirTags settings

Like AirPods, after unloading the box on AirTag, you can set Air-Tag with one tap. Each AirTag can be customized with the name and description of the item.

AirTag ID restrictions

Each Apple ID can be associated with up to 16 AirTags, so you can track up to 16 items at a time.

AirTags privacy and security

Every AirTag you own is associated with your "Apple ID" and no one else can follow it. Location data and location history are not stored on AirTag. Devices that transmit lost AirTag location will remain anonymous, and each step of location data will be encrypted.

If your lost AirTag is retrieved by someone else's device, you can see its location on the map, but you will never know who the person who helped you find it. Due to end-to-end encryption, Apple can't see AirTag location either.

AirTag has a unique Bluetooth identifier, which rotates always, this feature ensures that you will never follow it everywhere.

Unwanted tracking restrictions

Apple has built-in security restrictions to prevent AirTag from being used for unnecessary privacy purposes.

If another AirTag owned by someone appears in your possession and travels with you for some time, your "iPhone" will send you an alert to let you know that an AirTag has been detected nearby, which will prevent someone from passing this plant. If you return to your home address or frequently visited location, you will receive an AirTag warning with you.

When this happens, you will see a notification that says "AirTag Found", and you can tap a notification to disable AirTag. If you are attaching AirTag to the item you want to borrow, you can choose to turn off the one-day "AirTag Detected" notification. If it is a family member, you can turn off "Security Notification" for those in the "Family Sharing" group.

- How to disable anonymous AirTags that are available to you to prevent tracking

The AirTag warning received will only be valid when AirTag is separated from its owner, so you don't have to worry about friends or family members with AirTag nearby.

AirTag, which has been away from its owner for three days, will make a noise every time it leaves to remind itself of its existence.

Share airtag

If you plan to share an item via AirTag with others, you may disable the security alert if someone shares it with someone in the "Family Sharing" group. If it does not belong to your family, the person borrowing the item may temporarily disable the alarm.

Apart from disabling the security alarm, no other activity can share AirTag with others. Only you can use you "Find My" app to track AirTags linked to "Apple ID". You can't give tracking access to others, so spouses can't track each other's stuff, and parents can't track children's stuff.

Travel via AirTag

If you plan to use AirTag while traveling, you should be aware of certain limitations. For example, Precision Finding will not be available in certain countries (such as Russia, Indonesia, and Argentina), and the list is provided in our AirTags travel guide.

Track pets and children

Apple has designed AirTags to track items, and Apple does not recommend using them to track pets or children. To keep the child's attention, Apple recommends using "Family Settings" Apple Watch.

AirTag NFC shortcut

Apple shortcuts can use AirTag's built-in NFC chip to start automation. Users can create a touch screen by tapping the top of the "iPhone" enabled NFC on the white plastic side of AirTag.

AirTag Accessories

If you need a retainer, key fob, or another AirTag accessory to attach your AirTag to your item, we have a dedicated AirTag guide, which provides great options.

How to replace AirTag battery

AirTag uses CR2032 battery-shaped batteries, which have a service life of at least one year before they need to be replaced. No one needs to replace the battery right now, but if you need a new battery, it's easy to replace a new battery.

CR2032 batteries are standard batteries and can be purchased on Amazon. Each battery is worth $ 1. You can also purchase them at most economy stores. After installing the new battery, follow the steps below to install it:

1. Press AirTag stainless steel support.
2. When pressed, rotate counterclockwise until the lid stops rotating.

3. Divide the two halves of the AirTag.

4. Remove the old battery and insert the new battery in the same direction, facing upwards. When the battery is fully charged, you will hear a ringing sound.

5. Insert the rest of the AirTag stainless steel and make sure the three tabs on the cover match the spaces in the AirTag.

6. Rotate the cover clockwise until it stops.

You can check AirTag battery capacity in "Find my app". When the battery is low, you will receive a notification on your iPhone telling you it's time to replace the battery.

How to get AirTag into lost mode

Apple AirTag is a small coin-based tool that can be connected to things like keys and wallets so that these apps can be tracked in the "Find Me" app via the Bluetooth device next to the Apple device.

You can use the "Items" tab on "Find My Items" to track "AirTags", like Apple devices, if the device is lost, you can put it in "lost mode" to recover it. If there is an AirTag nearby, it will connect to an Apple device via Bluetooth to transfer its location, and the iPhone 11 and 12 have a direct search function that uses the U1 chip to locate items placed in the wrong location nearby.

You can still use the "Find My" app to track external AirTags, but they won't depend on your device's Bluetooth signal. In contrast, the "Find My" network uses almost one million Apple devices to help you find AirTag.

However, if AirTag is not close and there is no Apple in the zone where it is located, "Find My Name" will only tell you where it last appeared on the map. In this case, you can put AirTag in lost mode. This way, if someone touches something with NFC with an NFC or Android device, they can help return it to you. This is how it works.

How to mark AirTag as unavailable

1. Launch the "Find My Own" app on your iPhone.
2. Click on an item.
3. Click the AirTag you want to mark as missing.

4. Swipe down on the card, then under "Lost Mode", click Enable.

5. Click to continue.
6. Enter your phone number in the input field and click Next.

7. Switch the switch next to "Notify when received" and customize the missing message when someone receives an item. Please note that if AirTag is not in the device range, you can customize the message only and then enable "discovery notification".

8. Click to activate.

Now that AirTag is marked lost, anyone who finds it can move it to an NFC-enabled phone or Android phone, and they will see a notification linking it to a website that contains your lost message and phone number URL. With the help of "Find My Network", you can also see the transfer location via other people's devices.

Exactly how to get AirTag on "Find my" on iPhone

Apple AirTag is a small button-built tool designed to link to items such as keys and wallets so that these apps can be hunted down using Apple-enabled Bluetooth on Apple's "Find Me" app.

If you have just set up a new AirTag, you will want to know how to follow it to get attachments where they are misplaced. If your iPhone or iPad is running iOS 14.5 / iPadOS 14.5 or later, you can use the "Find My Own" app to retrieve the lost AirTag connected to your Apple ID. That's all.

How to check the location of AirTag items

In "Find my app", click "Items", then click the item you want to find.

- If an item can be found, it will appear on the map. You will see the updated location and timestamp under the product name.
- If you do not find the item, you will see when it was installed and when it was stored. To be notified when a notification is available, enable "Notify when received" under "Notifications".

How to make AirTag play audio

If there is an AirTag nearby, you can play audio to make it easier to find.

1. In "Find my app", click on "Project".
2. Click the AirTag you want to play.

3. Click to play audio.

To pause the sound before it automatically ends, click "Stop Sound."

You can also get a map of the current or final location map of the item. If you have a supported phone and are close to your AirTag, you can find its exact location.

How to play audio on AirTag

Apple AirTag is a small button-built tool designed to link to items such as keys and wallets so that these apps can be hunted down using Apple-enabled Bluetooth on Apple's "Find Me" app.

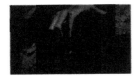

If you have set AirTag and attached it to an item, if it is placed in the wrong place, you can track that item in the Find My app. The "Find" function uses a Bluetooth signal from a lost AirTag to transfer its location to its owner, and to devices with a U1 chip, it has a direct search function that allows you to accurately determine the location of the AirTag range.

However, what should I do if I can see AirTagged objects, or am I close by? For example, if you know that you have lost the keys behind the sofa, it is still difficult to find them. Fortunately, Apple has already considered this, which is why you can allow AirTag to play audio that will help you find it.

How to make AirTag play audio

If there is an AirTag nearby, you can play audio to make it easier to find.

1. In "Find my app", click on "Project".
2. Click the AirTag you want to play.

3. Click to play audio.

To pause the sound before it automatically ends, click "Stop

Sound." You can also take AirTag and squeeze it to stop it.

Use Siri to play audio

If you ask Siri to find my [item] or play audio on my [item], Siri will record AirTag and make a sound to receive it.

You can also get a map of the current or final location map of the item, and if you have a supported iPhone and are close to AirTag, you can find its exact location.

How to install AirTag to get mine on iPhone

Apple AirTag is a small button-built tool designed to link to items such as keys and wallets so that these apps can be hunted down using Apple-enabled Bluetooth on Apple's "Find Me" app.

If you have a new AirTag, you need to set it up and configure it for use. Before performing this operation, please be sure to update your iPhone or iPad to iOS 14.5 or iPadOS 14.5 respectively. You can check your iOS version in Settings -> General -> Software Updates.

How to install AirTag on iPhone and iPad

1. Make sure your "iPhone" is turned on and the home screen is displayed.
2. If the battery label is not removed from AirTag, move it closer to the iPhone
3. On the card from the screen, click "Connect."

4. Choose a name from the list, or click "Custom Name" to enter a name and select emoji, then click "Continue."

5. Click "Continue" to register the item on your Apple ID, then click "Finish".

How to add AirTag to "Find Mine"

If necessary, you can subscribe to the new AirTag directly from the "Find My" app.

1. Start "I found" and click on "Project".
2. Scroll to the bottom of the "Items" menu and click "Add New Item".
3. Click Add AirTag and follow the instructions on the screen.

If AirTag is already registered in someone else's "Apple ID", they need to disconnect it before installing it. They can do the following in "Find Me" on their "iPhone": tap the item, then tap AirTag to delete it. Place the item next to the iPhone, then tap Delete item, then follow the instructions on the screen.

How to check AirTag battery life

The AirTag is fitted out with a CR2032 battery, and Apple claims its service life is at least one year, so you don't have to concern about the battery in the AirTag often.

If you want to know if it can withstand it, or you are worried that it will go down if it is not right, you can easily check the AirTag battery level in the "I Found" app.

1. Open "Find my app" and tap on the "Project" tab.
2. Click the name of the AirTag you want to check.

3. Battery life is listed under the AirTag name and location, so you can see it at a glance.

The battery icon doesn't give a certain percentage, but it's the same as the iPhone's battery and will expire over time.

You do not need to pay too much attention to the battery because the iPhone will notify you when the battery starts to drop, so you can replace it. For instructions on changing the AirTag battery, we offer you a detailed and useful battery-operated process.

How to reset AirTag to factory settings for others to use

When you set up AirTag, it will be linked to your Apple ID, which means it is connected to your "Apple ID" and other people cannot use it without resetting it.

By taking the following steps, resetting is as simple as removing AirTag from the "Apple ID":

1. Open the Find My app.
2. Tap AirTag to be removed by selecting its name from the list.
3. Swipe up to display full AirTag settings.
4. Click "Delete Item".

5. Click "Delete" and then click "Delete" again to open a window.

After you complete this process, the AirTag ID will be cleared, and you can give it to someone else to set up and use their account.

Unfortunately, if AirTag is not in its Bluetooth range when deleted from the account, it will not be able to register, so a manual reset is required. If you find that someone has associated you with their ID but deleted AirTag from their account, please follow the steps below to physically reset AirTag:

1. Press AirTag stainless steel support.
2. When pressed, rotate counterclockwise until the lid stops

rotating.

3. Divide the two halves of the AirTag.

4. Remove the battery.
5. Replace the battery.
6. Press the battery down until it sounds loud.
7. After the sound is finished, repeat the process four times, remove the battery and replace it, and press the battery until you hear the sound.

8. You need to hear a total of five sounds to ensure that Air-Tag is reset.
9. After completing this process, re-attach the lid to AirTag, and align the three tabs on the cover with the three spaces on AirTag.
10. Press the cover down until it makes a noise, then turn the cover clockwise until it locks in place.

To avoid the heavy physical reset process, it is best to make sure that the person who gave you the AirTag is within the range of Bluetooth to remove it properly from the account, as this is an easy way to clear AirTag ownership and transfer it to people.

How to turn off AirTag project security alert

Apple's AirTag object tracker is designed to attach personal items, such as keys, wallets, wallets, etc. so that the owner can tag these items and track them with an iPhone or iPad if they are not properly positioned.

After setting up AirTag on Apple's "Find Me" network, only the owner can track it using his or her iOS device. Apple also implemented an anti-tracking system. If an anonymous AirTag appears to be accompanying you, you will receive a notification that the owner is aware of your location.

At the same time, Apple recognizes that in some cases, users may want to share their AirTag-based items (for example, a set of keys) with friends or family. Therefore, if you are sharing an AirTag with someone else in the owner's "Family Sharing", you can pause or disable the security alert to prevent a family member's "iPhone" from being detected as "malicious tracking."

Additionally, if AirTag is borrowed from someone who is not in the "Family Sharing", the borrower may choose to suspend the safety features of his or her iOS device or disable it completely. The following steps show how you can do this last one.

Before proceeding, please remember that as long as the "Item Security Alert" is disabled, the owner of the anonymous object can see your location, and you will not be notified if an unknown item is found to be traveling with you.

1. Unveiling the "I Found " app on your iPhone or iPad.

2. Tap the "I" tab in the lower right angle of the screen.
3. Change the switch next to "Object Security Notice"
4. Click Disable to confirm.

Please note that this setting only affects the device you are currently using, so if you do not want to receive security alerts on another device, you need to repeat these steps on that device.

What to do if you find an AirTag that makes noise

Apple's AirTag tracker is designed to use "Find My Network" on iOS devices to store tags on personal items (such as keys, wallets, backpacks, suitcases, etc.).

If AirTag is separated from its owner for some time, it will make a noise to notify people nearby. If you receive an AirTag after hearing the sound, you can take the following steps to return it to its official owner.

1. Tap and hold on top of an iPhone or NFC-enabled smartphone to fix it on AirTag white surface.
2. Tap the notification displayed on the device screen. This will open the website and give you details about AirTag, including its serial number.

3. If the owner notices that AirTag is missing, the message can be displayed with information on how to contact the owner, allowing you to contact the owner to let them know you have found their AirTagged item.

AirTag can only be used to track items via iPhone or iPad via the Find the My app. Apple sells one "AirTags" for $ 29, or four "AirTags" for $ 99. For more information about the AirTag item tracker, please check out our dedicated guide.

There is a problem with the AirTag security function

While AirTags are good, they are not perfect, especially in terms of safety features.

After looking forever, Apple AirTag is now open to everyone. Air-Tag is a small Apple tracker that can help you make sure you don't lose important items like keys, wallets, purses, backpacks, etc. However, Apple wants to make it clear that AirTag is specifically designed to track items, not people or pets (although speaking of technology, you may be at risk).

AirTag is not the only thing tracker on the market. You can compete with Tile Mate and Tile Pro's Tile, even Chipolo One's Chipolo. However, one thing that makes Apple's AirTags different is that Apple used other anti-tracking features, while competitors found nothing in this.

However, in the opinion of "Washington Post", while we may recommend Apple and use other security features with AirTags, there is room for improvement.

So, what's wrong with AirTag's safety work? There are a few things. Let's go inside.

An audible alarm sounded just three days later

I did not check myself, but according to a Washington Post report, as long as AirTag is separated from its owner, it will not start crying until three days after it is separated. As soon as AirTag starts ringing (about 60 decibels (not too big)), it will keep ringing for 15 seconds, then be quiet for a few hours. After that, she cried for another 15 seconds. Frankly, 60 decibels is not too big (this is a typical conversation noise between two people). The sound can be easily applied by applying pressure to a white plastic cover attached to the speaker. If AirTag is hidden, the victim may not hear it at all.

Now, if you haven't found it yet, it will take one person three days to follow someone else. And only if AirTag is separated from the owner, a three-day count applies - if one stays with the stalker (unfortunately but true), then the countdown will be reset every time they return home, thus making the countdown useless.

Kann Drance, Apple's vice president of iPhone marketing, said the three-day period was because the company was measuring how these alarm bells could affect users who simply borrowed family members' bags or simply left things behind. Apple hopes to measure how notifications are issued by accidental tracking.

Despite being compared to the competition, Apple has even added these features for complete safety, which is quite good, but some improvements can be made. Maybe you have reduced the alarm time from 72 hours to a more reasonable time, such as 12 hours or less? As the countdown is reset whenever AirTag reconnects with the owner, the result may be better. This can be a hardware problem, but if the alarm catches the victim's attention, the alarm should exceed 60 decibels.

Only the iPhone will receive a warning that "AirTag was found to be with you"

Although the AirTag sound alarm seems to work only after three days of separation from the owner, there is another way to remind you that AirTag non-tracking is following you, but only if you have an iPhone 6s. This method works even more. The big problem with this is, what about people who don't use an iPhone?

If someone plans to use AirTag to track others, and the victim does not have an iPhone, then they will never know they are being tracked. While Android users who get AirTag in lost mode can use the built-in NFC to return AirTag to its owner, if you use Android, you can't decide if you have AirTag this way. This is a huge security hole. At the moment, it seems to be the only way to fix this problem is to buy the best iPhone, which is not a good solution at all.

If you think half (or more) of people are using Android and can't notify Android users that their AirTag has been tracked in some way, this is a huge security hole. If Apple wants to go all out to ensure that AirTag can't be used to track others, it needs to consider integrating some kind of notification system with Android devices. After all, it is impossible to reach anti-tracking measures with AirTags again, right?

Having an iPhone does not help to accurately detect the hidden AirTag

Whether using the iPhone 6s or higher also get the "AirTag detected value" warning we just mentioned, which is incomplete. Yes, because it will appear on your iPhone, it's hard to miss the warning. After a few hours, as your iPhone's Bluetooth connection always requires an AirTag nearby, it should appear. It will detect that AirTag is traveling with you and separated from its owner.

When you click on this warning, it will launch the "I Found" app and notify you on the screen that "the owner can see your current AirTag location". Then you can use this hidden AirTag to view a map that contains all the places you've been. From there, "Find Me" will tell you how to temporarily mute the alarm, or disable AirTag by simply removing the battery.

However, if you want to know where AirTag is in your body, it will be a very difficult task. The button allows you to play audio from a private AirTag to help you find it, but this may not always work 100%, depending on external factors such as width and wireless interference. Unfortunately, the exact look feature available to iPhone 11 and iPhone 12 owners cannot be used to detect anonymous AirTags. Unfortunately, because victims should be able to use these features to help them locate and remove unwanted AirTags.

Another dangerous security hole is that there is an option in "Find My App" to disable all "Project Security Notifications" and there is no need to enter a PIN or password. Think about it — if a person is in an abusive relationship, they may not be able to fully control their electronic devices. The abuser can simply plug in the victim's phone and block all the alarms, leaving them completely unaware, as these alarms are monitored throughout the day.

TIPS AND TRICKS

AirTag and project tracking are compatible. With direct tracking and a huge "Find My Network", and backed by more than one million Apple devices, Apple's product tracker looks better than its competitors. And it has become a favorite of many people, especially considering its seamless integration into the Apple ecosystem. That said, if you want to maximize the benefits that AirTag brings, please try the following 10 AirTag tips and tricks.

In addition to seamless connectivity and object tracking, AirTag also provides the necessary security so that criminals can use it to track your location. To me, this is probably the most impressive feature of Apple's product tracker. In this guide, I have discussed the benefits of improving your device tracking experience and security features that can prevent anyone from tracking your whereabouts. So, without wasting any time, let's take a look at Air-Tag's performance.

Use direct search to find the wrong AirTag

In addition to Bluetooth, the AirTag is also equipped with Apple's U1 ultra-wideband chip. Additionally, if you have an iPhone 11 or iPhone 12 series device that comes with a U1 chip, you can take advantage of a simple option called "Precision Find". This will help you determine the distance and direction of the lost AirTag.

The iPhone uses input from the accelerometer, gyroscope, and camera to direct AirTag's exact location using tactile feedback, sound, and visuals. Having the latest iPhone brings one of Air-Tag's simplest tips and tricks.

To use the specific search feature, open "Find My App" and go to the "Projects" tab. Next, select the AirTag you want. After that, click the "Find Near" option and follow the on-screen instructions to find the missing item.

Let AirTag play audio for easy access

If your bad AirTag is nearby, you can play audio on the object tracker. Loud noise will make it easier to get AirTag. To do this, launch the "Find My" app on your iPhone and go to the "Project" tab. After that, select Lost AirTag and click the "Play Audio" button. After receiving AirTag, please click "Stop Sound" to stop Air-Tag audio.

Check the battery life of your AirTag

AirTag comes with a CR2032 battery that can be replaced by the user. Although Apple claims that the CR2032 battery can be used normally for one year, it may not be enough for the way you use the device. Therefore, it is best to track AirTag battery life to see how much juice is left in the tank. I know this may seem like a small thing, but in the long run, it will be one of the best AirTag strategies.

We have written a detailed guide on how to check AirTag battery life, you can read the linked article for all the information. In addition, we have introduced steps to replace the AirTag battery in this guide.

Replace your AirTag battery

Replacing the AirTag battery is very easy. So, if you find that the product tracker battery is low, you can easily replace it. It is important to note that you can purchase CR2032 batteries on Amazon AirTag Amazon. Additionally, you can also purchase batteries from most offline stores. Therefore, when the battery needs to be replaced, it will not cost much to buy a new CR2032 battery.

Here are some popular AirTag CR2032 battery packs on Amazon:

- ECB CR2032 3V lithium battery: 10 packs $ 5.99
- Duracell CR2032 button battery with hot coating: 4 packs $ 6.34
- Amazon Basics CR2032 button battery: 4 pieces for $ 5.49
- Energizer CR2032: 4 button packs $ 4.49

Steps to replace AirTag battery

First, we need to remove the existing AirTag battery. Press the stainless steel back on the AirTag with two fingers. While pressing, turn on the cross until the lid stops rotating. Now, separate the two parts and remove the old battery. After that, replace it with a new one.

Make sure the new battery status is the same (lookup). Next, lower the AirTag stainless steel back, making sure the three tabs on the cover match the spaces. Yes, you have successfully replaced the AirTag battery.

Put your AirTag in lost mode

When AirTag is nearby, with the help of Bluetooth and Precision Finding (for iPhone 11 and iPhone 12), an item tracker can be easily found. However, when the item tracker is out of range, you should rely on "Find My Network" to recover lost AirTag. Remember, if there is no Apple device in the area where your AirTag is located, you can only view the location of the tracker.

Open the "Find My Own" app on your iPhone and go to the "Project" tab. After that, select AirTag and swipe up the card to access the "Lost Mode" section. Next, click Allow. Next, you can enter your phone number and a custom message, which will be displayed when someone finds your lost AirTag. Finally, click "Activate" to enable "Lost Mode" on your AirTag.

After marking your AirTag as lost, anyone with an iPhone or Android device that supports NFC can access your lost messages and choose to return the tracking item to you. This will make you a good Samaritan, this is one of the best tips and tricks for AirTag.

Safely return AirTag to its official owner

If you find lost AirTag, you can scan the tracker to access the owner's contact details. It is noteworthy that you need to use an iPhone or Android device that supports NFC to view detailed information.

Just press and hold the white side of the AirTag on the back of your iPhone or NFC Android device. After that, tap the notification displayed on the device. Now, the website will open with detailed information about AirTag, including its product number and contact details of the owner. In addition, you can also see a missing message and phone number, which will enable you to contact the right owner.

Factory reset your Apple AirTag

When you set up AirTag with your iPhone, it will link you to your Apple ID. Therefore, you need to reset the item tracker to factory settings before handing it over to someone else or selling it. It's easy to reset AirTag when you're on Bluetooth, and there are some useful and deceptive suggestions in the arsenal.

• Reset AirTag with "Find My App"

Navigate to the "Project" tab in the "I Found" app and select the Air-Tag you want to delete. After that, swipe up to display AirTag settings, then tap the "Delete It" option. After that, confirm that you want to delete AirTag from your account in the pop-up window.

• Manually reset AirTag

Remember, if you are not in your AirTag Bluetooth range when you delete AirTag from your account, it will not be able to register. Therefore, AirTag will need to be reset manually. To do this, press the side of the stainless steel. While pressing down on the stainless steel side, rotate the cover against the clock until it stops rotating.

Next, separate the two parts of the AirTag, and remove the battery. After that, return the battery inside and press the battery down until it sounds loud. After the sound is finished, repeat the same process four times. Yes, you need to remove and replace the battery, then press the battery until you hear five beeps.

After completing the process, be sure to return the metal cover to the AirTag in its place. Next, align the three tabs on the cover with the three locations in the device tracker. Finally, press down until it makes a noise, then turn it clockwise to lock it firmly in place. That's all. You have now reset AirTag manually.

You can also use this method to disable AirTag that travels with you and easily set it up as your own. Resetting AirTag yourself is a tedious task. Therefore, always make sure that when the device tracker is in Bluetooth range, the person who gave you AirTag has deleted it from their account.

Turn off the AirTag project security warning

For security reasons, iOS 14 only allows owners to use the "I Found" app to track AirTag. In addition, it also has an anti-tracking system that will alert you when an unknown AirTag appears to be traveling with you. It informs you that the owner of the AirTag can see your location, and this is a well-thought-out idea.

But what if you want to share your AirTag tracking material with friends or family? You do not want to disable warnings security eye? You probably will. Don't worry, iOS lets you pause your security alert so that your beloved iPhone or iPad doesn't detect unwanted AirTag.

Do note that for as long as Item Safety Warnings are paused, the owner of an unknown AirTag can see your whereabouts. Also, bear in mind that you won't be given alerts when you move in the opposite direction with that unknown item on you.

Open the Find My app on your iPhone or iPad and go to the "I" tab. Now, turn off the closure next to Item Safety Warnings.

Next, a popup will seem on the screen warning you that "the holder of an unknown will be able to see your whereabouts and you will no longer receive warnings when an unknown item is found moving with you." Tap on "Deactivate" to authorize the action.

Stop People from Stalking You Using an AirTag

The Apple AirTag originates with a built-in safety feature that stops the item tracker from being used to track your location. Thus, no one can put an AirTag in your furniture and keep track of your whereabouts without your awareness. This is one of the top AirTag tips and tricks I want everyone to be aware of for their safety.

If your iOS device spots an AirTag that doesn't belong to you moving with you for a prolonged period, it will alert you with a warning message. Now, you can take the needed action and use our detailed guide to deactivate an AirTag found moving with you in a few easy steps.

Access AirTag's Hidden Developer Menu

This isn't the best AirTag tip or trick and may get detached in an upcoming update. But, in what possibly will be the icing on the cake for the folks who love to tinker with yet-to-be-rolled-out features, Apple has a top-secret AirTag developer mode accessible via the Find My app. The hidden developer mode shows a variety of data along with the sliders to adjust things like dot-moving pictures for precision finding, background color, and more.

So if you need to enable AirTag developer mode and play about with various dials and sliders, go ahead and follow our linked guide. There's even a battery saver 'Eco' mode and an interesting 'Interactive Mode' hidden in the designer menu.